Mothers!

CARTOONS BY WOMEN

Are you my mother?

SUZY BECKER

Edited by
Roz Warren

The Crossing Press, Freedom, CA 95019

Mothers! is dedicated with
love to my son Thomas.

———————

A million thanks to Elaine Goldman Gill for mothering this book along,
and to Mom and Alvia for mothering me along.

ISBN 0-89594-611-4

Cartoonists

The Joy of Pregnancy and Childbirth

© 1980 T.O. SYLVESTER

"I feel another Grade A Large coming on."

Anne Gibbons

Madam Rosa

I see diapers, many, many diapers.

..and if it's a girl, will you name her Thelma or Louise?
©Anne Gibbons

'When the baby comes out, I can play with it – and then I can put it back'

Signe Wilkinson

Male pregnancy may become viable option

Male pregnancy is scientifically possible and government should consider regulating the practice now to protect men who might want to give birth, a Princeton University professor said. Molecular biologist Lee Silver, who testified last week before a state panel investigating advanced reproductive techniques in response to New Jersey's Baby M surrogate mother-

Baby Frenzy

"Beautiful, beautiful, jelly mommy"

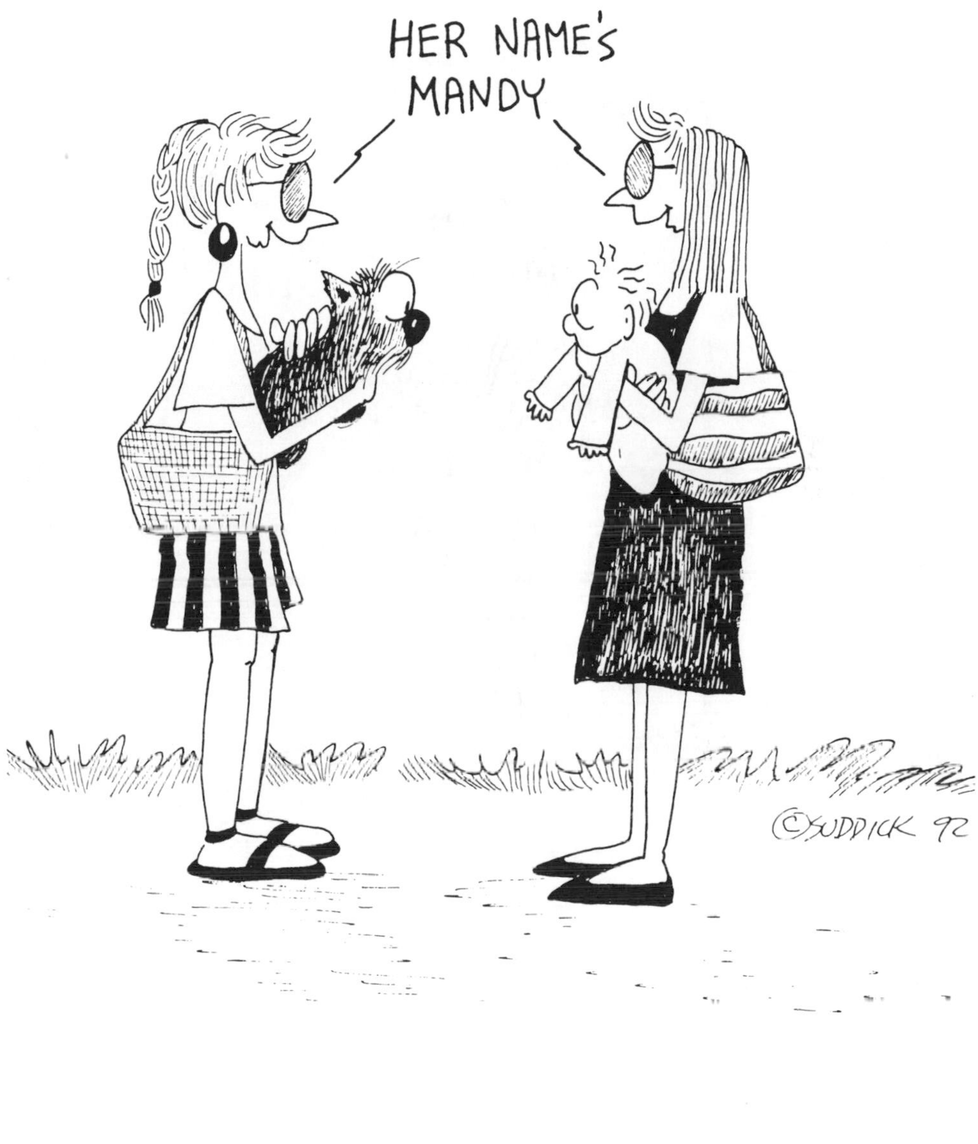
HER NAME'S MANDY
©SUDDICK 92

Viv Quillin

MY COLLEAGUES AND I HAVE DISCOVERED A HEIGHTENED PERIOD OF ACTIVITY BETWEEN THE HOURS OF 4 AND 7 p.m. WHICH IS COMMON TO THE SPECIES AND VARIES ONLY IN DURATION AND INTENSITY. WE CALL THIS AGITATION, "BABY FRENZY".

'I wish I could do that'

Anne Gibbons

Gail Machlis

The NEW MOTHER'S GUIDE to LEISURE

♥

with index to 4 star restaurants welcoming newborns

A BLANK BOOK

Suzy Becker

In the news today, President Bush signed a bill providing federal funding for the Massage for Mothers program, a nationwide service that will offer six yearly massages free for all mothers. The bill will go into effect immediately.

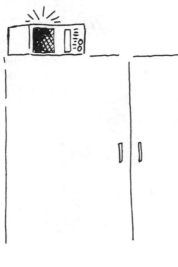

gmachlis ©89
Gail Machlis

MOM MAKES THE MOST OF A TRAFFIC JAM

Anne Gibbons

'I'm thrilled she's started to use the potty'

Ros Asquith

Diane Germain

I TOOK THE PROMOTION BECAUSE WITH THE PAY
INCREASE I CAN PUT THE KIDS IN A MORE "HOMEY" DAYCARE..

The Art
of
Motherhood

LEMIEUX
4·6

Kathryn LeMieux

PERHAPS YOU COULD TRY TO MAKE YOUR MORNING
GOODBYES A LITTLE MORE POSITIVE, MRS. KRANTZ.

Martha Gradisher

Anne Gibbons

 was referenced above; the comic reads:

the art of motherhood by cherry

SEPTEMBER BLUES... OR
THE PEAS ARE ALWAYS GREENER...

REWRITE THIS NOW!

To Do
1. umm
2. umm
3. umm
4. umm
5. umm
6. umm
7. umm

SIGH! I MISS MY KIDS SO MUCH! I FEEL SO GUILTY LEAVING THEM... IF I WERE HOME WE'D TAKE WALKS, GO TO PLAYGROUP, HAVE REAL QUALITY TIME TOGETHER! I'D WEAR OLD JEANS, COOK GOURMET DINNERS, HAVE LUNCH WITH FRIENDS, SIGH!!

SIGH! I MISS MY JOB SO MUCH!! I FEEL SO BORING STAYING HOME...IF I WORKED PEOPLE WOULD RESPECT MY INTELLIGENCE, CALL ME BY MY REAL NAME, NOT "MOMMY." I'D WEAR NICE CLOTHES THAT NO ONE WOULD WIPE THEIR NOSE ON AND HAVE LUNCH WITH CLIENTS WHO COULD FEED THEMSELVES. HECK, I MIGHT EVEN MISS THE KIDS!! SIGH!

COOKIE!

AW, MA PLEASE!

© 1991 MARCIE CHERRY

Margie Cherry

Jan Eliot

Jan Eliot

THE ADVENTURES OF
WIMP MOM

There are definitely times of the day when one's three-year-old may be in a horrible mood.

Who knows what the Tough Mom might do to stop that sort of thing?

NOW YOU STAY IN YOUR ROOM UNTIL YOU'RE READY TO ACT LIKE A **HUMAN BEING, PAL!!!!**

If you are a Wimp Mom, perhaps you will try to distract your kid in a calm, soothing manner.

Honeybunch, let's go over to the couch and *READ ABOUT DINO-SAURS!*

ALL YOU WANT TO KNOW ABOUT DINOSAURS

You are lucky if this works for ten seconds

"Dinosaurs were very, very big."

Often, you will only find yourself in deeper and hotter water.

NO, THEY WEREN'T!!!...

What a wimpy, wimpy Mom.

O.K., they weren't big. They were as tiny as peas.

Roz Chast

P. Chst

"I'M NOT VERY GOOD AT JUGGLING CAREER AND FAMILY. I'VE DROPPED SEVERAL HUSBANDS."

Martha Campbell

GRADISHER...
Martha Gradisher

"AND QUIT CALLING ME YOUR WICKED BIOLOGICAL MOTHER."

Martha Campbell

"I LIVE IN A SINGLE-PARENT HOUSEHOLD TOO."

Martha Campbell

'No wonder they cry . . . how would you like to be three foot tall, constantly falling over, flat broke and unable to speak the language'

BED TIME STORIES

Stephanie Piro

Heimlich's
Mother's
Maneuvers

Jan Eliot

Jan Eliot

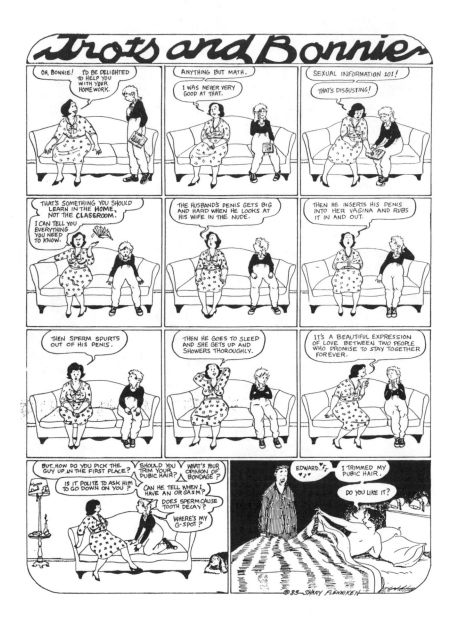

HEIMLICH'S MOTHER'S MANEUVERS

The Skinned-Knee
Maneuver—

Go on and on about person's
bravery. Then place the
hugest **Band-Aid** you can
find over the icky area.

*What a BIG BOY
you are!*

The Anti-Nausea
Maneuver ~

Cajole person into eating a
small piece of plain chicken
and sipping some warm,
flat ginger ale.

*Have just a
little*

The Splinter-Removal
Maneuver ~

Have person look at the
ceiling and think happy
thoughts while you dig
around with a needle.

Roz Chast

The EGG

one from the memoirs

I was barely eleven when my mother handed me a copy of the Reader's Digest...

I AM JANE'S WOMB?

Then we had a little talk...

IT'S TIME WE HAD A LITTLE TALK...

She explained how every month an egg is released...

...FROM A WOMAN'S OVARY...

If she had sex with her husband at just the right time his sperm would fertilize her egg and...

A BABY WOULD START TO GROW!!

But if the egg wasn't fertilized it would come out her vagina. This was men-stroo-ation.

And soon it would be happening to me!!

It all sounded okay except the end part where I find the egg in my underpants.

© Noreen Stevens 1990

Noreen Stevens

Jan Eliot

Lynda Barry

Jan Eliot

MOMMA'S FAULT!

Wendy Weber likes to keep part of the day to *herself*... *a private* time, when she can loose the reins of *domesticity* and continue working on her thesis......

...or, sometimes, if the Muse fails:

Oh **Momma!** I don't **care!** I'm gonna **keep** this **BABY**...and I'm gonna do it **RIGHT!** I'm gonna be a <u>real</u> mother!

GASP: Why, Donna!

I'm gonna be a **mother** who's **ALWAYS** <u>there</u>...to share **EVERY** joy...to wipe away **EVERY** tear!

GASP: Oh Honey!

NOT like **YOU**, Momma! CHOKE! Where **WERE YOU** all my life?

You were **ALWAYS** someplace else.... ...**ALWAYS** your bureau came **FIRST!**

All my life, I **NEVER** came home to the smell of **BAKING** :SOB:

Oh Donna! SOB!

I tried...

...**Gaad** knows I tried!

I wanted you to feel **FREE**, Donna! ..to lead your own life.. I didn't want to **PRY**, to **FUSS**...to **SMOTHER!**

cont.→

© Posy Simmonds

Posy Simmonds

Noreen Stevens

My Mother's Motto...

"I can't cook, I can't sew...
but I'm A Great Companion!"

Stephanie Piro

STRIP T's by Stephanie ©92

Are You
Sure
You're a Good
Mother?

Caryn Leschen

Jan Eliot

..love 'em and leave 'em! That's what I like to do!
Men???
Grandchildren.
KAR
©Anne Gibbons

THE WAKE UP CALL

40

Barbara Slate

Jan Eliot

Jackie Smith

WATCHING VISITING DAUGHTER'S
HOME VIDEO FOR THE FIRST TIME...

WATCHING VISITING DAUGHTER'S
HOME VIDEO FOR THE HUNDRETH TIME...

Nicole Ferentz

Roberta Gregory

"He told me I'd end up like my
Mother... I told him that
was the best compliment
he could have paid me..."

Stephanie Piro

Mom... even though I'm far away, and we don't get to spend a lot of time together, I just think you should know...

I still want to borrow your clothes

Joann Palanker

He was still very attached to
his mother...

R. PICCOLO © '92

Rina Piccolo

Visit to Mom

Jennifer Camper

Jan Eliot

*IT'S TRUE, TOO! I'M NOT MAKING THIS UP!

Nina Paley

I HAVE A SPASTIC COLON, TOO!

IF I DRINK TOO MUCH COFFEE,

LIVE WITH TOO MUCH STRESS,

OR TOUCH THOSE DAIRY PRODUCTS—

VOILÁ!

I HAVE THE EQUIVALENT OF

AN ABDOMINAL CHARLEYHORSE!

Sigh...

BUT EVERY ONCE IN AWHILE, WHEN I'M LAYING THERE WITH MY HOT WATER BOTTLE, TRYING TO DEEP BREATHE AND IGNORE THE PAIN...

I THINK ABOUT MOM.

MOM

AND I REALIZE THAT MY WEAK BLADDER, LACTOSE INTOLERANCE AND SPASTIC COLON CONNECT ME TO HER, AND TO ALL OF THE GENERATIONS THAT HAVE COME BEFORE...

GAWD!

WAYASSISMARIA!

ERG!

FOR MOM, WHO PASSED ON, QUIRKS AND ALL, JULY 1990.   ©JACKIE URBANOVIC   1991

If you enjoyed this book you may enjoy Roz Warren's other publications:

Women's Glib, A Collection of Women's Humor: Cartoons, stories and poems by America's funniest women wits that will knock you off your chair laughing.

Kitty Libber, Cat Cartoons by Women: Hilarious feline funnies by all the best women cartoonists.

Women's Glib, Cartoon Engagement Calendar 1994: Hilarious quotes, cartoons and light verse by leading women humorists for every week of the year. $9.95

These books are available at your local bookstore or you can order directly from us. Use the coupon below, or call toll-free 800-777-1048. Please have your VISA or Mastercard ready.